Green STEAM

EARTH-FRIENDLY
EARTH DAY
CRAFTS

Veronica Thompson

Lerner Publications ◆ Minneapolis

Lerner Publications Company
A division of Lerner Publishing Group, Inc.
241 First Avenue North
Minneapolis, MN 55401 USA

For reading levels and more information, look up this title at www.lernerbooks.com.

Main body text set in Avenir LT Pro 12/16.
Typeface provided by Linotype AG.

Photo Acknowledgments
The images in this book are used with the permission of: © cosmaa/Shutterstock Images, p. 1 (Earth icon); © Stilesta/Shutterstock Images, pp. 1, 3, 9, 11, 13, 15, 17, 19, 21, 23, 24, 25, 27, 28 (border design element); © ineskoleva/iStockphoto, p. 4 (calendar); © pearleye/iStockphoto, p. 4 (Earth); © wavebreakmedia/Shutterstock Images, p. 5 (kids); © wildpixel/iStockphoto, p. 5 (Earth Day); © AKIRA_PHOTO/Shutterstock Images, p. 6 (top); © Gts/Shutterstock Images, p. 6 (bottom); © Lubava/Shutterstock Images, p. 7 (hot glue gun); © Saliy Serge/Shutterstock Images, p. 7 (art supplies); Veronica Thompson, pp. 8, 9 (top), 9 (center), 9 (bottom), 10, 11 (top), 11 (center top), 11 (center bottom), 11 (bottom), 12, 13 (top), 13 (center), 13 (bottom), 14, 15 (top), 15 (center), 15 (bottom), 16, 17 (top), 17 (center), 17 (bottom), 18, 19 (top), 19 (center), 19 (bottom), 20, 21 (top), 21 (center), 21 (bottom), 22, 23 (top), 23 (bottom), 24 (top), 24 (center), 24 (bottom), 25 (top), 25 (bottom), 26, 27 (top), 27 (center), 27 (bottom), 28 (top), 28 (bottom); © Curly Pat/Shutterstock Images, pp. 9, 11, 13, 15, 17, 19, 21, 23, 24, 25, 27, 28 (design element); © karen roach/Shutterstock Images, p. 29 (top); © Chones/Shutterstock Images, p. 29 (center); © Butterfly Hunter/Shutterstock Images, p. 29 (bottom); © Protasov AN/Shutterstock Images, p. 30; © Happetr/Shutterstock Images, p. 31; © malerapaso/iStockphoto, p. 32 (top); Courtesy Veronica Thompson, p. 32 (bottom)

Front cover: Veronica Thompson (main); © cosmaa/Shutterstock Images (Earth icon)
Back cover: © Curly Pat/Shutterstock Images (background design element); © Stilesta/Shutterstock Images (border design element)

Library of Congress Cataloging-in-Publication Data

The Cataloging-in-Publication Data for *Earth-Friendly Earth Day Crafts* is on file at the Library of Congress.
978-1-5415-2420-0 (lib. bdg.)
978-1-5415-2779-9 (pbk.)
978-1-5415-2426-2 (eb pdf)

Manufactured in the United States of America
1-44508-34764-4/23/2018

CONTENTS

Scan QR codes throughout for step-by-step pictures of each craft.

EARTH DAY

Did you know our planet gets its own special day? Every year, people celebrate Earth Day on April 22. Many people plant trees and pick up litter in honor of this holiday. People also discuss the importance of recycling and reducing waste. Making crafts out of repurposed items is one way to reduce waste.

Get ready to reuse and revamp everyday objects to celebrate Earth!

April

22

Earth Day

CHOOSING MATERIALS

When you're gathering things to repurpose, it's okay to be picky. For example, avoid cardboard with food or grease stains on it. Ask an adult before reusing something that isn't in the recycling bin. The item may be serving another purpose already!

CLEAN MACHINE

Reused materials may carry germs or other substances. Give these materials a good scrub before you craft with them! Put a jar in the dishwasher, wipe off old shoes, and ask an adult to wash fabric before beginning a project.

STAY SAFE!

Some crafts in this book require sharp or hot tools. Ask for an adult's help when using these items:

- blender
- hot glue gun
- oven

CONFETTI PAPER

Recycling paper helps save trees! Convert scraps of old homework, junk mail, and more into colorful sheets of patterned homemade paper.

MATERIALS
- recycled paper
- scissors
- liquid measuring cup
- large bowl
- water
- blender
- glitter
- old 8" × 10" picture frame
- old window screen or recycled, fine plastic mesh
- hot glue gun & glue sticks
- spoon
- towel
- small plastic storage tub slightly smaller than the old picture frame

1 Cut recycled paper into small strips. Place 8 cups of strips in the bowl. Set a small handful of strips aside. These will remain dry. Fill the bowl with water and soak the strips overnight.

2 In the morning, scoop the wet strips into a blender. Leave the water in the bowl. **Blend** the wet strips a bit. Add ½ cup of water and some glitter, then blend again. You've made paper **pulp**!

3 Remove the glass and backing from the picture frame. Glue the old window screen or plastic mesh to the frame. Place the frame over the plastic tub.

4 Spoon the pulp onto the screen, spreading it into an even layer. Sprinkle the dry paper strips from step 1 onto the pulp and pat them down.

5 Place a towel on a flat, sunny surface. Then place the tub and screen on the towel. The water from the pulp will drip into the tub. You will be left with a colorful sheet of paper!

Scan the QR code for more photos.

PAPER BLOOM BARRETTE

Revamp paper into a flower you can wear in your hair!

MATERIALS
~ repurposed colored paper
~ scissors
~ hot glue gun & glue sticks
~ barrette or hair clip

1 Cut three circles from paper. Cut out three smaller green ovals. Fold each oval in half to make leaves.

2 Cut fringe around each circle. Make long cuts but stop before reaching the circle's center.

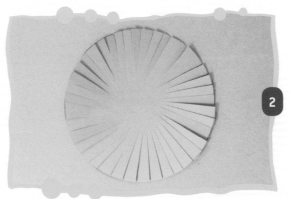

3 Have an adult help curl each circle's fringe using a scissor blade. Slide the blade up the fringe while pressing the other side with your thumb. Curl all fringe on one circle in the same direction. Repeat to curl the fringe on the other two circles.

4 Place a dot of hot glue in the center of one curled circle, with the fringe facing up. Set another curled circle on top of the glue, with the fringe facing up. Repeat this step with the last circle.

5 Glue the leaves onto the barrette, being careful not to glue it closed. Glue the circles on top of the leaves. When the glue dries, your bloom is ready to wear!

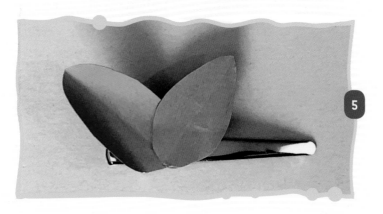

BEE TOWNHOME

Turn household items into a townhome for bees!

MATERIALS
- 80–100 recycled large plastic straws
- scissors
- bowls
- reusable facial tissue box cover
- hot glue gun & glue sticks
- paint
- paintbrush

STEM Takeaway
Bees pollinate plants that produce dazzling flowers and delicious fruits and veggies.

1 Wash and dry the recycled straws. Cut each straw in half. Place the pieces in bowls for easy reach.

2 Stand the tissue box cover on one small side. Glue a straw piece along one inner, bottom corner.

3 Glue straw pieces to the bottom of the box in a row. Glue more pieces above them to make another row. Repeat until the box is full or you're out of straws.

4 Paint the sides of the box to look like a house. Then set your bee townhome up outside! Place it on a level surface and somewhere with dappled sunlight and minimal wind.

SWAP IT!
Swap the facial tissue box cover with any repurposed box, such as a small storage tub.

FOREVER FLOWER BOWL

Repurpose leftover clay to create a pretty peony bowl that celebrates Earth's beauty.

MATERIALS
~ oven-safe glass bowl
~ leftover bits of oven-bake clay
~ plastic wrap
~ rolling pin
~ empty water or soda bottle
~ oven mitts

1 Turn the bowl upside down.

2 Shape a bit of clay into a ball. Place it between two sheets of plastic wrap. Roll the clay into circle that is about a ¼-inch (0.6 cm) thick.

3 Remove the clay circle from the plastic wrap. Place the circle on top of the bowl.

4 Repeat step 2 using more clay. Remove the clay from the plastic wrap and press the rim of the open bottle into the clay like a cookie cutter several times to make small circles. Shape these circles to look like petals then press them around the clay circle on the bowl.

5 Repeat step 4 to make more layers of petals in different colors.

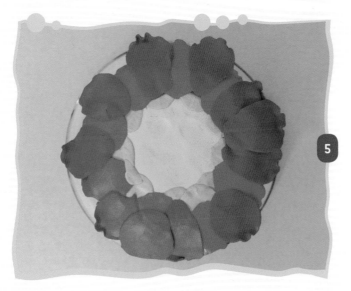

6 Have an adult help you place the glass bowl and clay in the oven for fifteen minutes at 275°F (135°C). Once the clay cools, remove it from the glass bowl.

RAINBOW CLUTCH

Follow a few simple steps to turn an old placemat into a colorful clutch.

STEM Takeaway
Rainbows form when rain and sunlight combine in a certain way.

MATERIALS
- ~ old round placemat
- ~ office clips, paper clips, or hair clips
- ~ red, orange, yellow, green, blue, and indigo craft paint
- ~ paintbrushes
- ~ hot glue gun & glue sticks
- ~ scissors
- ~ two repurposed, flat refrigerator magnets

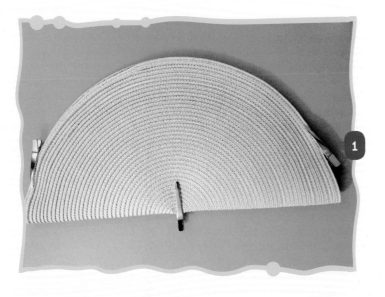

1 Fold the placemat in half. Use clips to hold it closed.

2 On one side, paint a thick red arc near the curved edge of the placemat.

3 Repeat step 2 with the orange, yellow, green, blue, and indigo paint. Paint each new arc under the previous one. When the first side dries, paint matching arcs on the other side.

4 Glue the curved edges of the placemat together, but leave a 5-inch (13 cm) opening at the top of the arc.

5 Glue the magnets across from each other inside the opening. Make sure they **attract** each other to keep the clutch closed!

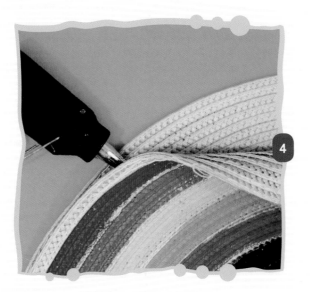

SWAP IT!
Staple the sides of the purse closed in step 4 instead of gluing.

I ♥ EARTH JOURNAL

Turn old pieces of paper into a journal and help save Earth's trees!

MATERIALS

- ~ 10–25 sheets of recycled construction paper, printer paper, or notebook paper with one blank side
- ~ double-stick tape
- ~ hole punch
- ~ ruler
- ~ cardboard gift box or empty cereal box
- ~ scissors
- ~ duct tape in various colors
- ~ string

1 Fold a sheet of paper in half crosswise so any type or images face inward. Place double-stick tape along the paper's inside edges and seal them shut. Repeat this step with all paper.

2 Punch two holes near the folded edge of each sheet of paper. Make sure that the holes are in the same place for all the sheets. Stack the folded sheets.

3 Cut two pieces of cardboard 6 by 9 inches (15 by 23 cm). These will be the front and back covers. Punch holes in them to match those made on the paper in step 2.

4 Wrap each cover in duct tape, except over the punched holes. Add a blue circle made of duct tape to **represent** Earth. Tape green shapes on it as land. Tape a heart near the planet to show your journal is Earth-friendly!

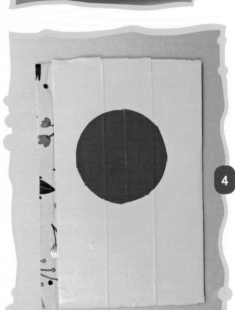

5 Stack the paper between the covers. Thread a piece of string through all top holes and tie it snug to the journal. Repeat with another piece of string and the bottom holes. Trim the extra string.

SWAP IT!
Swap out the colorful duct tape for paint or stickers!

MARINE MEMOS

Keep Earth's landfills from filling up by reusing paper scraps instead of tossing them. Turn a notebook into a colorful sea scene using these materials.

MATERIALS

- recycled large plastic bottle cap or circular container lid
- recycled construction paper
- scissors
- recycled notebook
- glue stick
- ruler
- stickers
- markers
- paper scraps in a variety of colors

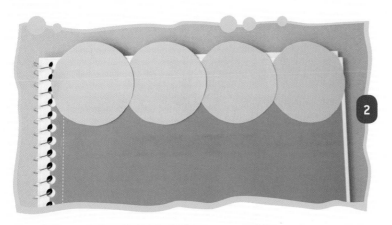

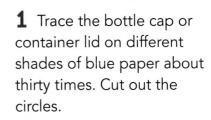

1 Trace the bottle cap or container lid on different shades of blue paper about thirty times. Cut out the circles.

2 Glue the circles on the top two-thirds of the notebook cover in overlapping rows. This is the ocean water. It's okay if the circles spill over the cover's edges.

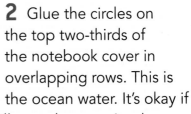

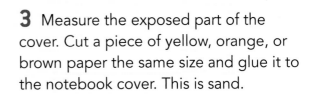

3 Measure the exposed part of the cover. Cut a piece of yellow, orange, or brown paper the same size and glue it to the notebook cover. This is sand.

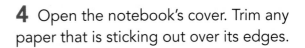

4 Open the notebook's cover. Trim any paper that is sticking out over its edges.

5 Add to your ocean scene. Cut coral reefs, fish, or sea plants out of scrap paper and glue them on. Apply stickers of sea creatures, add drawings, and more!

SHARK SHOES

Celebrate the sea by revamping old shoes to feature one of its most famous animals, the shark!

MATERIALS
~ old canvas or fabric shoes
~ gray, white, black, pink, red, blue, and green fabric paint
~ paintbrushes

STEM Takeaway
Sharks lived on Earth 200 million years before dinosaurs.

1 Remove the shoelaces.

2 Paint a gray half circle on the outer side of each shoe. Add a fin in the middle of each circle.

3 Next, make the shark faces. Paint a white triangle into the front edge of each shark for mouths.

Shark Shoes continued on next page

4 Outline each white triangle in black and paint lines for teeth. Add one black dot above each mouth to make eyes.

5 Paint a pink half circle on each heel. Paint a white arc above each circle.

6 Paint a gray arc above each white arc on the heel.

7 Paint a small red half circle inside each pink half circle. These are the sharks' mouths.

8 Add a black dot on either side of the gray arcs for eyes. Add two short black lines at the top center of each gray arc. These are shark **nostrils**!

9 Outline the top of the pink arcs in black. Paint white triangles below these lines to make teeth.

10 Paint the rest of the shoes blue. Add fun details such as air bubbles and seaweed!

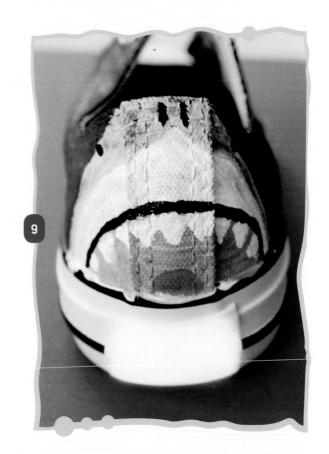

SWAP IT!
Swap the shoes for an old cotton or canvas backpack, T-shirt, or pair of jeans.

SWIRLY PLANTERS

Planting something is a great way to celebrate Earth Day!
Using recycled materials to do so is even more Earth friendly.

MATERIALS
- plastic wrap
- small plastic storage tub
- water
- recycled glass jars with lids
- old nail polish in several colors
- paint stir stick or small wooden dowel
- large bowl
- 3 quarts potting soil
- large bowl
- ⅓ cup of leftover coffee grounds
- herb seeds (basil, thyme, and cilantro recommended)

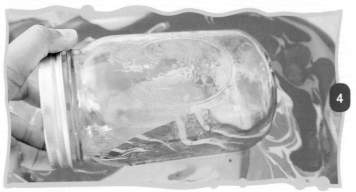

PLANTERS

1 Cover your work surface in plastic wrap.

2 Fill the plastic tub halfway with water. Set it on the plastic wrap. Place the lidded jars next to the tub.

3 Pour a bit of each nail polish into the water. Swirl the polish around using the stir stick or dowel.

4 Working quickly, roll one jar carefully along the surface of the water. The nail polish should stick to the jar in swirls. Set the jar on its lid and out of the way on the plastic wrap.

5 Repeat step 4 for all jars, then allow them to dry.

Swirly Planters continued on next page

SWAP IT!
Swap the jars for recycled clear plastic containers.

POTTING

6 Pour the soil into the bowl. Mix in the coffee grounds.

7 Discard the jar lids and fill the jars with the soil mixture. Poke your finger into the soil in each jar to make a small hole, then drop in a pinch of seeds. Cover the holes with more soil mixture.

8 Water the jars and place them near a sunny window. Wait and watch your herbs grow!

ODDS & ENDS

Craft materials and a little creativity can give new life to all kinds of old or recycled materials. What else can you repurpose?

PLASTIC BOTTLES

Cut sections out of plastic bottles and fill them with birdseed to make simple bird feeders.

MILK JUGS

Poke holes in the lids of recycled plastic milk jugs to turn them into watering cans.

PLASTIC BAGS

Weave and braid plastic bags into a cool tote!

EGG CARTONS

Cut the cups from egg cartons to look like flowers. Glue the blooms to recycled straw stems.

CLEAR GLASS CONTAINERS

Clean old glass containers well, then add rocks and water to make tiny fish tanks.

PLASTIC LIDS

Glue colorful recycled plastic lids to cardboard to create a bright rainbow, ocean scene, and more.

GLOSSARY

attract: to draw by appeal to natural interest or to pull to or draw toward oneself or itself

blend: to mix two or more things together so they combine

convert: to turn something into something else

creativity: the use of the imagination to think of new ideas

nostrils: the two openings in the nose that an animal breathes and smells through

pollinate: to carry pollen between flowers to fertilize them or produce seeds

pulp: any soft, wet mixture

represent: to be a sign or symbol of something

repurposed: given a new purpose or use

revamp: to remake or redesign

species: one of the groups into which animals and plants are divided

FURTHER INFORMATION

BOOKS

Bullard, Lisa. *Go Green for Earth Day.*
Minneapolis: Lerner Publications, 2019.
Learn about recycling, saving energy, and more in this fun, illustrated book about Earth Day.

Scheunemann, Pam. *Trash to Treasure: A Kid's Upcycling Guide to Crafts: Fun, Easy Projects with Paper, Plastic, Glass & Ceramics, Fabric, Metal, and Odds & Ends.*
Minneapolis: Scarletta Junior Readers, 2013.
Find ways to turn trash into useful crafts! Step-by-step instructions, photos, and tips will help you as you create.

Thompson, Veronica. *Earth-Friendly Animal Crafts.*
Minneapolis: Lerner Publications, 2019.
Get inspired to upcycle recycled items into crafts for and featuring all kinds of animals!

WEBSITES

Britannica Kids: Earth Day
https://kids.britannica.com/kids/article/Earth-Day/390242
Read more about Earth Day and how people around the world celebrate this holiday.

PBS: Crafts for Kids–All Earth Day Crafts
http://www.pbs.org/parents/crafts-for-kids/category/holiday/earth-day/
Choose from a large list of Earth-friendly crafts! Each craft has photos and easy-to-follow instructions.

***National Geographic Kids*: Save the Earth**
https://kids.nationalgeographic.com/explore/celebrations/earth-day/#earth-day-cleanup.jpg
Discover actions you can take to help protect and clean up Earth.

INDEX

ABOUT THE AUTHOR/ PHOTOGRAPHER

Veronica Thompson lives in a little brownstone in Brooklyn, New York, with her two puppies and wonderful husband. She spends her days crafting for her website, makescoutdiy.com, and building websites.